Contents

Articles of Agreement

This Agreement is made the ______________________ 20 ________

Between **The Employer** ____

____

______________________________________ (Company No. ____________)[1]

of/whose registered office is at ______________________________________

____

____

And **The Contractor** ____

____

______________________________________ (Company No. ____________)[1]

of/whose registered office is at ______________________________________

____

____

[1] Where the Employer or Contractor is not a company incorporated under the Companies Acts, delete the references to Company number and registered office.

Recitals

Whereas

First the Employer wishes to have the following work carried out[2]:

____

____

at ____

____ ('the Works')
under the direction of the Architect/Contract Administrator referred to in Article 3;

Second the Employer has had the following documents prepared which show and describe the work to be done:

the drawings numbered/listed in ______________________ ('the Contract Drawings')[3][4]

a Specification ('the Contract Specification')[3]

Work Schedules[3]

which for identification have been signed or initialled by or on behalf of each Party and those documents together with the Conditions and, if applicable, a Schedule of Rates as referred to in the Third Recital (collectively 'the Contract Documents') are annexed to this Agreement[5];

Third the Contractor has supplied the Employer with a copy of the priced Contract Specification or Work Schedules or provided a Schedule of Rates[3];

Fourth for the purposes of the Construction Industry Scheme (CIS) under the Finance Act 2004, the status of the Employer is, as at the Base Date, that stated in the Contract Particulars;

Fifth for the purposes of the Construction (Design and Management) Regulations 2007 (the 'CDM Regulations') the status of the project that comprises or includes the Works is stated in the Contract Particulars;

Sixth where so stated in the Contract Particulars, this Contract is supplemented by the Framework Agreement identified in those particulars;

Seventh the Supplemental Provisions identified in the Contract Particulars apply;

---

[2] State nature and location of intended works.
[3] Delete as appropriate.
[4] State the identifying numbers of the Contract Drawings or identify the schedule of drawings or other document listing them.
[5] Where a Contract Document has been priced by the Contractor it is that version of the document that should be annexed.

Articles

Now it is hereby agreed as follows

Article 1: Contractor's obligations

The Contractor shall carry out and complete the Works in accordance with the Contract Documents.

Article 2: Contract Sum

The Employer will pay the Contractor at the times and in the manner specified in the Conditions the VAT-exclusive sum of

____

____________________ (£ ____________________.______) ('the Contract Sum')

or such other sum as shall become payable under this Contract.

Article 3: Architect/Contract Administrator

For the purposes of this Contract the Architect/Contract Administrator[6] is

____

of ____

____

or, if he ceases to be the Architect/Contract Administrator, such other person as the Employer shall nominate for that purpose (such nomination to be made within 14 days of the cessation), provided that no replacement Architect/Contract Administrator appointed for this Contract shall be entitled to disregard or overrule any certificate, opinion, decision, approval or instruction given by any predecessor in that post, save to the extent that that predecessor if still in the post would then have had power under this Contract to do so.

Article 4: CDM Co-ordinator

The CDM Co-ordinator for the purposes of the CDM Regulations is the Architect/Contract Administrator

(or)[7] ____

of ____

____

or, if he ceases to be the CDM Co-ordinator, such other person as the Employer shall appoint pursuant to regulation 14(1) of those regulations.

---

[6] Where the person named in Article 3 is entitled to the use of the name 'Architect' under and in accordance with the Architects Act 1997 delete 'Contract Administrator': in all other cases delete 'Architect'. Where 'Architect' is deleted here, the expression 'Architect' shall be deemed to have been deleted throughout this Contract; where 'Contract Administrator' is deleted here, the expression 'Contract Administrator' shall be deemed to have been deleted throughout.

[7] Insert the name of the CDM Co-ordinator only where the Architect/Contract Administrator is not to fulfil that role, and that of the Principal Contractor only if that is to be a person other than the Contractor. If the project that comprises or includes the Works is not notifiable under the CDM Regulations 2007 – see the Contract Particulars (Fifth Recital), delete Articles 4 and 5 in their entirety.

Article 5: Principal Contractor

The Principal Contractor for the purposes of the CDM Regulations is the Contractor

(or)[7] ____

of ____

____

or, if he ceases to be the Principal Contractor, such other contractor as the Employer shall appoint pursuant to regulation 14(2) of those regulations.

Article 6: Adjudication

If any dispute or difference arises under this Contract either Party may refer it to adjudication in accordance with clause 7·2.[8]

Article 7: Arbitration

Where Article 7 applies[9], then, subject to Article 6 and the exceptions set out below, any dispute or difference between the Parties of any kind whatsoever arising out of or in connection with this Contract shall be referred to arbitration in accordance with Schedule 1 and the JCT 2005 edition of the Construction Industry Model Arbitration Rules (CIMAR)[10]. The exceptions to this Article 7 are:

- any disputes or differences arising under or in respect of the Construction Industry Scheme or VAT, to the extent that legislation provides another method of resolving such disputes or differences; and
- any disputes or differences in connection with the enforcement of any decision of an Adjudicator.

Article 8: Legal proceedings[9]

Subject to Article 6 and (where it applies) to Article 7, the English courts shall have jurisdiction over any dispute or difference between the Parties which arises out of or in connection with this Contract.

---

[8] As to adjudication in cases where the Employer is a residential occupier within the meaning of section 106 of the Housing Grants, Construction and Regeneration Act 1996, see the Guidance Notes.

[9] If it is intended, subject to the right of adjudication and exceptions stated in Article 7, that disputes or differences should be determined by arbitration and not by legal proceedings, the Contract Particulars **must** state that the arbitration provisions of Article 7 and Schedule 1 apply and the words "do not apply" **must** be deleted. If the Parties wish any dispute or difference to be determined by the courts of another jurisdiction the appropriate amendment should be made to Article 8 (see also clause 1·7).

[10] See the Guidance Notes.

Contract Particulars

Note: An asterisk* indicates text that is to be deleted as appropriate.

Clause etc.	*Subject*	
Fourth Recital and Schedule 2 (paragraphs 1·1, 1·2, 1·5, 1·6, 2·1 and 2·2)	Base Date	______________________
Fourth Recital and clause 4·2	Construction Industry Scheme (CIS)	Employer at the Base Date * is a 'contractor'/is not a 'contractor' for the purposes of the CIS
Fifth Recital	CDM Regulations[11]	the project * is/is not notifiable
Sixth Recital	Framework Agreement (if applicable) *(State date, title and parties.)*	______________________ ______________________ ______________________ ______________________
Seventh Recital and Schedule 3	Supplemental Provisions *(Where neither entry against an item below is deleted, the relevant paragraph applies.)*	
	Collaborative working	Paragraph 1 * applies/does not apply
	Health and safety	Paragraph 2 * applies/does not apply
	Cost savings and value improvements	Paragraph 3 * applies/does not apply
	Sustainable development and environmental considerations	Paragraph 4 * applies/does not apply
	Performance Indicators and monitoring	Paragraph 5 * applies/does not apply

[11] A project is not notifiable under the CDM Regulations where it is not likely to involve more than 30 days, or 500 person days, of construction work or it is being carried out for a residential occupier as a purely domestic project.

	Notification and negotiation of disputes	Paragraph 6 * applies/does not apply
	Where paragraph 6 applies, the respective nominees of the Parties are	Employer's nominee ____________________ ____________________ Contractor's nominee ____________________ ____________________ or such replacement as each Party may notify to the other from time to time
Article 7	Arbitration *(If neither entry is deleted, Article 7 and Schedule 1 do not apply. If disputes and differences are to be determined by arbitration and not by legal proceedings, it must be stated that Article 7 and Schedule 1 apply.)*[12]	Article 7 and Schedule 1 (*Arbitration*) * apply/do not apply
1·1	CDM Planning Period[13]	shall mean the period of ____________________* days/weeks * ending on the Date for Commencement of the Works/ * beginning/ending on ____________________ 20 ______
2·2	Date for Commencement of the Works	____________________
2·2	Date for Completion	____________________

[12] On factors to be taken into account by the Parties in considering whether disputes are to be determined by arbitration or by legal proceedings, see the Guidance Notes. See also footnote [9].

[13] Under the CDM Regulations 2007 every client is expressly required to allocate sufficient time (the CDM Planning Period) prior to the commencement of construction to enable contractors and others to carry out necessary CDM planning and preparation. There may be cases where that planning and preparation needs to be completed earlier than the Date for Commencement of the Works.

2·8	Liquidated damages	at the rate of £ ______________ per ______________[14]
2·10	Rectification Period *(The period is 3 months unless a different period is stated.)*	______________________ months[15] from the date of practical completion
4·3	Percentage of the total value of work etc. *(The percentage is 95 per cent unless a different rate is stated.)*	______________________ per cent[15]
4·4	Percentage of the total amount to be paid to the Contractor *(The percentage is 97½ per cent unless a different rate is stated.)*	______________________ per cent[15]
4·8·1	Supply of documentation for computation of amount to be finally certified *(The period is 3 months unless a different period is stated.)*	______________________ months[15] from the date of practical completion
4·11 and Schedule 2	Contribution, levy and tax changes	Schedule 2 (*Fluctuations Option*) applies[16]
4·11 and Schedule 2 (paragraph 13)	Percentage addition for Fluctuations Option	______________________ per cent
5·3·2	Contractor's insurance: injury to persons or property – insurance cover *(for any one occurrence or series of occurrences arising out of one event)*	£ ______________________
5·4A, 5·4B and 5·4C	Insurance of the Works etc. – alternative provisions[17]	* Clause 5·4A (*Works insurance by Contractor in Joint Names*) applies/ * Clause 5·4B (*Works and existing structures insurance by Employer in Joint Names*) applies/ * Clause 5·4C (*Existing structures insurance by Employer in own name*) applies

---

[14] Insert 'day', 'week' or other period.
[15] An insertion is needed here only if the default position is not to apply. If no retention is required, insert '100' in the entries for clauses 4·3 and 4·4.
[16] Delete if the contract period is of such limited duration as to make the provision inappropriate.
[17] Delete as appropriate.
Depending on the nature of the project and insurance available, the Parties may use:
i) clause 5·4A on its own (where the Works are not an extension to or an alteration of an existing structure);
ii) clause 5·4B on its own (where the Works are an extension to or an alteration of an existing structure and the Employer can obtain the insurance in Joint Names in compliance with clause 5·4B); or
iii) clause 5·4C together with clause 5·4A (where the Works are an extension to or an alteration of an existing structure and where the Employer is a residential occupier and cannot obtain the insurance in Joint Names in compliance with clause 5·4B). See the Guidance Notes.

5·4A·1 and 5·4B·1·2	Percentage to cover professional fees *(If no other percentage is stated, it shall be 15 per cent.)*	______________ per cent
7·2	Adjudication[18]	The Adjudicator is ______________
	Nominating body – where no Adjudicator is named or where the named Adjudicator is unwilling or unable to act (whenever that is established)[19] *(Where an Adjudicator is not named and a nominating body has not been selected, the nominating body shall be one of the bodies listed opposite selected by the Party requiring the reference to adjudication.)*	* Royal Institute of British Architects * The Royal Institution of Chartered Surveyors * Construction Confederation * National Specialist Contractors Council * Chartered Institute of Arbitrators
Schedule 1 (paragraph 2·1)	Arbitration[20] – appointor of Arbitrator (and of any replacement)[21] *(If no appointor is selected, the appointor shall be the President or a Vice-President of the Royal Institute of British Architects.)*	President or a Vice-President: * Royal Institute of British Architects * The Royal Institution of Chartered Surveyors * Chartered Institute of Arbitrators

[18] The Parties should either name the Adjudicator and select the nominating body or, alternatively, select only the nominating body. The Adjudication Agreement (Adj) and the Adjudication Agreement (Named Adjudicator) (Adj/N) have been prepared by JCT for use when appointing an Adjudicator.

[19] Delete all but one of the nominating bodies asterisked.

[20] This only applies where the Contract Particulars state (against the reference to Article 7) that Article 7 and Schedule 1 (*Arbitration*) apply.

[21] Delete all but one of the bodies asterisked.

Attestation

Note on Execution

This Agreement should be executed by both the Employer and the Contractor either under hand or as a deed. As to the main factor relevant to that choice, see the Guidance Notes.

Execution under hand

If this Agreement is to be executed under hand, use the form set out on the following page. Each Party or his authorised representative should sign where indicated in the presence of a witness who should then sign and set out his name and address.

Execution as a Deed

If this Agreement is to be executed as a deed, each Party should use the relevant form marked 'Execution as a Deed' in accordance with the notes provided.

Other forms of Attestation

In cases where the forms of attestation set out are not appropriate, e.g. in the case of certain housing associations and partnerships or if a Party wishes an attorney to execute this Agreement on his behalf, the appropriate form(s) may be inserted in the vacant space opposite and/or below.

As witness

the hands of the Parties
or their duly authorised representatives

Signed by or on behalf of the Employer ______________________________

in the presence of: ______________________
witness' signature

____
witness' name

____
witness' address

____

Signed by or on behalf of the Contractor ______________________________

in the presence of: ______________________
witness' signature

____
witness' name

____
witness' address

____

Notes on Execution as a Deed

1 For the purposes of execution as a deed, two forms are provided for execution, one for the Employer and the other for the Contractor. Each form provides four methods of execution, **(A)** to **(D)**, for use as appropriate. The full name of the Employer or Contractor (whether an individual, a company or other body) should be inserted where indicated at the commencement of the relevant form. This applies irrespective of the method used.

2 For public and private companies incorporated and registered under the Companies Acts, the three principal methods of execution as a deed are:

(A) through signature by a Director and the Company Secretary or by two Directors;

(B) by affixing the company's common seal in the presence of a Director and the *Company* Secretary or of two Directors or other duly authorised officers; or

(C) signature by a single Director in the presence of a witness who attests the signature.

Methods **(A)** and **(C)** are available to public and private companies whether or not they have a common seal. (Method **(C)** was introduced by section 44(2)(b) of the Companies Act 2006.) Methods **(A)** and **(C)** are not available under companies legislation to local authorities or to certain other bodies corporate, e.g. bodies incorporated by letters patent or private Act of Parliament that are not registered under companies legislation and such bodies may only use method **(B)**.

3 Where method **(A)** is being used, delete the inappropriate words and insert in the spaces indicated the names of the two Directors, or of the Director and the Company Secretary, who are to sign.

4 If method **(B)** (affixing the common seal) is adopted in cases where either or both the authorised officers attesting its affixation are not themselves a Director or the *Company* Secretary, their respective office(s) should be substituted for the reference(s) to Director and/or to *Company* Secretary/Director. (In the case of execution by bodies that are not companies, the reference to "*Company*" under the second signature should be deleted where appropriate.)

5 Method **(C)** (execution by a single Director) has been introduced primarily, but not exclusively, for 'single officer' companies. The Director should sign where indicated in the presence of a witness who should then sign and set out his name and address.

6 Where the Employer or Contractor is an individual, he should use method **(D)** and sign where indicated in the presence of a witness who should then sign and set out his name and address.

Executed as a Deed by the Employer

namely [1] ____

(A) acting by a Director and the Company Secretary/two Directors **of the company** [2, 3]

________________________________ and ________________________________

(Print name of signatory) *(Print name of signatory)*

________________________________ ________________________________

Signature Director *Signature* Company Secretary/Director

(B) by affixing hereto the common seal **of the company/other body corporate** [2, 4]

in the presence of

____

Signature Director

____

Signature *Company* Secretary/Director

[Common seal of company]

(C) by attested signature of a single Director **of the company** [2, 5]

____

Signature Director

in the presence of

Witness' signature ____________________ *(Print name)* ____________________

Witness' address ____

(D) by attested signature **of the individual** [6]

____

Signature

in the presence of

Witness' signature ____________________ *(Print name)* ____________________

Witness' address ____

Note: The numbers on this page refer to the numbered paragraphs in the Notes on Execution as a Deed.

Executed as a Deed by the Contractor

namely [1] ______________________________

(A) acting by a Director and the Company Secretary/two Directors **of the company** [2, 3]

______________________________ and ______________________________

(Print name of signatory) *(Print name of signatory)*

______________________________ ______________________________

Signature Director *Signature* Company Secretary/Director

(B) by affixing hereto the common seal **of the company/other body corporate** [2, 4]

in the presence of

____

Signature Director

____

Signature *Company* Secretary/Director

[Common seal of company]

(C) by attested signature of a single Director **of the company** [2, 5]

____

Signature Director

in the presence of

Witness' signature ______________________________ *(Print name)* ______________________________

Witness' address ______________________________

(D) by attested signature **of the individual** [6]

____

Signature

in the presence of

Witness' signature ______________________________ *(Print name)* ______________________________

Witness' address ______________________________

Note: The numbers on this page refer to the numbered paragraphs in the Notes on Execution as a Deed.

Conditions

Section 1 Definitions and Interpretation

Definitions

1·1 Unless the context otherwise requires or the Agreement or these Conditions specifically provide otherwise, the following words and phrases, where they appear in capitalised form in the Agreement or these Conditions, shall have the meanings stated or referred to below:

Word or phrase	*Meaning*
Agreement:	the Articles of Agreement to which these Conditions are annexed, consisting of the Recitals, the Articles and the Contract Particulars.
All Risks Insurance[22]:	insurance which provides cover against any physical loss or damage to work executed and Site Materials and against the reasonable cost of the removal and disposal of debris and of any shoring and propping of the Works which results from such physical loss or damage but excluding the cost necessary to repair, replace or rectify: (a) property which is defective due to: (i) wear and tear, (ii) obsolescence, or (iii) deterioration, rust or mildew; (b) any work executed or any Site Materials lost or damaged as a result of its own defect in design, plan, specification, material or workmanship or any other work executed which is lost or damaged in consequence thereof where such work relied for its support or stability on such work which was defective[23]; (c) loss or damage caused by or arising from: (i) any consequence of war, invasion, act of foreign enemy, hostilities (whether war be declared or not), civil war, rebellion, revolution, insurrection, military or usurped power, confiscation, commandeering, nationalisation or requisition or loss or destruction of or damage to any property by or under the order of any government *de jure* or *de facto* or public, municipal or local authority, (ii) disappearance or shortage if such disappearance or shortage is only revealed when an inventory is made or is not traceable to an identifiable event, or (iii) an Excepted Risk.
Article:	an article in the **Agreement**.
Business Day:	any day which is not a Saturday, a Sunday or a Public Holiday.

[22] The definition of All Risks Insurance defines the risks for which insurance is required. Policies issued by insurers are not standardised and the way in which insurance for those risks is expressed varies.

[23] In any policy for All Risks Insurance taken out under clause 5·4A or 5·4B·1·2, cover should not be reduced by the terms of any exclusion written in the policy beyond the terms of paragraph (b) in this definition of All Risks Insurance; thus an exclusion in terms 'This Policy excludes all loss of or damage to the property insured due to defective design, plan, specification, materials or workmanship' would not be in accordance with the terms of those insurance clauses or of that definition. Wider All Risks cover than that specified may be available to Contractors, though it is not standard.

continued 1·1

CDM Co-ordinator:	the Architect/Contract Administrator or other person named in **Article 4** or any successor appointed by the Employer.
CDM Planning Period:	the minimum amount of time referred to in regulation 10(2)(c) of the CDM Regulations, as specified in the **Contract Particulars** (against the reference to **clause 1·1**).
CDM Regulations:	the Construction (Design and Management) Regulations 2007.
Conditions:	the clauses set out in sections 1 to 7, together with and including the Schedules hereto.
Construction Industry Scheme (or 'CIS'):	see the **Fourth Recital**.
Construction Phase Plan:	the plan prepared by the Principal Contractor, where the project is notifiable under the CDM Regulations and in order to comply with regulation 23, including any updates and revisions.
Contract Particulars:	the particulars in the **Agreement** and there described as such, including the entries made by the Parties.
Excepted Risks:	ionising radiations or contamination by radioactivity from any nuclear fuel or from any nuclear waste from the combustion of nuclear fuel, radioactive toxic explosive or other hazardous properties of any explosive nuclear assembly or nuclear component thereof, pressure waves caused by aircraft or other aerial devices travelling at sonic or supersonic speeds.
Fluctuations Option:	the provisions set out in **Schedule 2**.
Insolvent:	see **clause 6·1**.
Interest Rate:	a rate 5% per annum above the official dealing rate of the Bank of England current at the date that a payment due under this Contract becomes overdue.
Joint Names Policy:	a policy of insurance which includes the Employer and the Contractor as composite insured and under which the insurers have no right of recourse against any person named as an insured, or recognised as an insured thereunder.
Parties:	the Employer and the Contractor together.
Party:	either the Employer or the Contractor.
Provisional Sum:	includes a sum provided for work that the Employer may or may not decide to have carried out, or which cannot be accurately specified in the Contract Documents.
Public Holiday:	Christmas Day, Good Friday or a day which under the Banking and Financial Dealings Act 1971 is a bank holiday.[24]
Recitals:	the recitals in the **Agreement**.
Rectification Period:	the period stated as such period in the **Contract Particulars** (against the reference to **clause 2·10**).
Scheme:	Part 1 of the Schedule to The Scheme for Construction Contracts (England and Wales) Regulations 1998.

[24] Amend as necessary if different Public Holidays are applicable.

continued 1·1

Site Materials:	all unfixed materials and goods delivered to and placed on or adjacent to the Works which are intended for incorporation therein.
Specified Perils:	fire, lightning, explosion, storm, flood, escape of water from any water tank, apparatus or pipe, earthquake, aircraft and other aerial devices or articles dropped therefrom, riot and civil commotion, but excluding Excepted Risks.
Statutory Requirements:	any statute, statutory instrument, regulation, rule or order made under any statute or directive having the force of law which affects the Works or performance of any obligations under this Contract and any regulation or bye-law of any local authority or statutory undertaker which has any jurisdiction with regard to the Works or with whose systems the Works are, or are to be, connected.
VAT:	Value Added Tax.

Agreement etc. to be read as a whole

1·2 The Agreement and these Conditions are to be read as a whole but nothing contained in the Contract Drawings, the Contract Specification or the Work Schedules, nor anything in any Framework Agreement, shall override or modify the Agreement or these Conditions.

Headings, references to persons, legislation etc.

1·3 In the Agreement and these Conditions, unless the context otherwise requires:

·1 the headings are included for convenience only and shall not affect the interpretation of this Contract;

·2 the singular includes the plural and vice versa;

·3 a gender includes any other gender;

·4 a reference to a 'person' includes any individual, firm, partnership, company and any other body corporate; and

·5 a reference to a statute, statutory instrument or other subordinate legislation ('legislation') is to such legislation as amended and in force from time to time, including any legislation which re-enacts or consolidates it, with or without modification.

Reckoning periods of days

1·4 Where under this Contract an act is required to be done within a specified period of days after or from a specified date, the period shall begin immediately after that date. Where the period would include a day which is a Public Holiday that day shall be excluded.

Contracts (Rights of Third Parties) Act 1999

1·5 Notwithstanding any other provision of this Contract, nothing in this Contract confers or is intended to confer any right to enforce any of its terms on any person who is not a party to it.

Notices and other communications

1·6 Unless otherwise provided in these Conditions, any notice or other communication under this Contract may be given or served by any effective means to the recipient at the address specified in the Agreement or such other address as he shall notify to the other Party. If no such address is then current, the notice or other communication shall be treated as effectively given or served if addressed and sent by pre-paid post to the recipient's last known principal business address or (where a body corporate) its registered or principal office.

Applicable law

1·7 This Contract shall be governed by and construed in accordance with the law of England.[25]

---

[25] Where the Parties do not wish the law applicable to this Contract to be the law of England appropriate amendments should be made.

Section 2 Carrying out the Works

Contractor's obligations

2·1 ·1 The Contractor shall carry out and complete the Works in a proper and workmanlike manner and in compliance with the Contract Documents, the Construction Phase Plan (where applicable) and other Statutory Requirements, and shall give all notices required by the Statutory Requirements.

·2 Where and to the extent that approval of the quality of materials or of the standards of workmanship is a matter for the Architect/Contract Administrator's opinion, such quality and standards shall be to his reasonable satisfaction.

·3 The Contractor shall take all reasonable steps to encourage employees and agents of the Contractor and sub-contractors employed in the execution of the Works to be registered cardholders under the Construction Skills Certification Scheme (CSCS) or qualified under an equivalent recognised qualification scheme.

Commencement and completion

2·2 The Works may be commenced on and shall be completed by the respective dates stated in the Contract Particulars.

Architect/Contract Administrator's duties

2·3 The Architect/Contract Administrator shall issue any further information and instructions necessary for the proper carrying out of the Works, and shall issue all certificates required by these Conditions.

Correction of inconsistencies

2·4 Any inconsistency in or between the Contract Drawings, the Contract Specification and the Work Schedules shall be corrected and any such correction which results in an addition, omission or other change shall be treated as a variation under clause 3·6·1.

Divergences from Statutory Requirements

2·5 ·1 If the Contractor becomes aware of any divergence between the Statutory Requirements and the Contract Documents or between the Statutory Requirements and any instruction of the Architect/Contract Administrator, he shall immediately give to the Architect/Contract Administrator a written notice specifying the divergence.

·2 Provided the Contractor is not in breach of clause 2·5·1, the Contractor shall not be liable under this Contract if the Works do not comply with the Statutory Requirements to the extent that such non-compliance results from the Contractor having carried out work in accordance with the Contract Documents or any instruction of the Architect/Contract Administrator.

Fees or charges legally demandable

2·6 The Contractor shall pay any fees or charges (including any rates or taxes) legally demandable under any of the Statutory Requirements. Such fees and charges shall not be reimbursable to the Contractor by the Employer, unless otherwise agreed.

Extension of time

2·7 If it becomes apparent that the Works will not be completed by the Date for Completion stated in the Contract Particulars (or any later date fixed in accordance with the provisions of this clause 2·7) for reasons beyond the control of the Contractor, including compliance with any instruction of the Architect/Contract Administrator under this Contract not arising from a default of the Contractor, then the Contractor shall thereupon in writing so notify the Architect/Contract Administrator who shall, in writing, give such extension of time for *continued 2·7* completion as may be reasonable. Reasons within the control of the Contractor include any default of the Contractor, of others employed or engaged by or under him for or in connection with the Works or of any supplier of goods or materials for the Works.

Damages for non-completion

2·8 ·1 If the Works are not completed by the Date for Completion stated in the Contract Particulars or by any later Date for Completion fixed under clause 2·7 the Contractor shall pay or allow to the Employer liquidated damages at the rate stated in the Contract Particulars between such Date for Completion and the date of practical completion.

·2 The Employer may either deduct the liquidated damages from any monies due to the Contractor under this Contract (provided that a notice of deduction has been given pursuant to clause 4·5·2 or 4·8·3) or recover the liquidated damages from the Contractor as a debt.

·3 If the Employer intends to deduct any such damages from the sum stated as due in the final certificate, he shall additionally inform the Contractor, in writing, of that intention not later than the date of issue of the final certificate.

Practical completion

2·9 The Architect/Contract Administrator shall certify the date when in his opinion the Works have reached practical completion and the Contractor has complied sufficiently with clause 3·9·4.

Defects

2·10 If any defects, shrinkages or other faults in the Works appear within the Rectification Period due to materials, goods or workmanship not in accordance with this Contract the Architect/Contract Administrator shall notify the Contractor who shall make good such defects, shrinkages or other faults entirely at his own cost unless the Architect/Contract Administrator with the consent of the Employer shall otherwise instruct.

Certificate of making good

2·11 The Architect/Contract Administrator shall certify the date when in his opinion the Contractor's obligations under clause 2·10 have been discharged.

Section 3 Control of the Works

Assignment

3·1 Neither the Employer nor the Contractor shall, without the written consent of the other, assign this Contract or any rights thereunder.

Person-in-charge

3·2 The Contractor shall ensure that at all reasonable times he has on the site a competent person in charge and any instructions given to that person by the Architect/Contract Administrator shall be deemed to have been issued to the Contractor.

Sub-contracting

3·3 ·1 The Contractor shall not without the Architect/Contract Administrator's written consent sub-contract the whole or any part of the Works. Such consent shall not be unreasonably delayed or withheld but the Contractor shall remain wholly responsible for carrying out and completing the Works in all respects in accordance with clause 2·1 notwithstanding any such sub-contracting.

continued 3·3

·2 Where considered appropriate, the Contractor shall engage the Sub-Contractor using the JCT Short Form of Sub-Contract. It shall be a condition of any sub-contract that:

·1 the sub-contractor's employment under the sub-contract shall terminate immediately upon the termination (for any reason) of the Contractor's employment under this Contract;

·2 each party undertakes to the other in relation to the Works and the site duly to comply with the CDM Regulations[26];

·3 if by the final date for payment stated in the sub-contract the Contractor fails properly to pay any amount, or any part of it, due to the sub-contractor, the Contractor shall in addition to the amount not properly paid pay simple interest at the Interest Rate for the period until such payment is made; such payment of interest to be on and subject to terms equivalent to those of clauses 4·6 and 4·9 of these Conditions.

Architect/Contract Administrator's instructions

3·4 The Architect/Contract Administrator may issue written instructions and the Contractor shall forthwith comply with any so given or confirmed. If instructions are given orally the Architect/Contract Administrator shall, within 2 days, confirm them in writing.

Non-compliance with instructions

3·5 If within 7 days after receipt of a written notice from the Architect/Contract Administrator requiring compliance with an instruction the Contractor does not comply, the Employer may employ and pay other persons to execute any work whatsoever which may be necessary to give effect to that instruction. The Contractor shall be liable for all additional costs incurred by the Employer in connection with such employment and an appropriate deduction shall be made from the Contract Sum.

Variations

3·6 ·1 The Architect/Contract Administrator may, without invalidating this Contract, issue instructions requiring an addition to, omission from, or other change in the Works or the order or period in which they are to be carried out.

·2 The Architect/Contract Administrator and the Contractor shall endeavour to agree a price prior to the Contractor carrying out the instruction.

·3 Failing any agreement under clause 3·6·2 any instructions issued under clause 3·6·1 shall be valued by the Architect/Contract Administrator on a fair and reasonable basis using any relevant prices in the priced Contract Specification/Work Schedules/Schedule of Rates, and the valuation shall include any direct loss and/or expense incurred by the Contractor due to the regular progress of the Works being affected by compliance with the instruction.

Provisional Sums

3·7 The Architect/Contract Administrator shall issue instructions in regard to the expenditure of any Provisional Sums included in the Contract Documents and such instructions shall be agreed or valued in accordance with clause 3·6·2 or 3·6·3.

Exclusion from the Works

3·8 The Architect/Contract Administrator may (but shall not unreasonably or vexatiously) issue instructions requiring the exclusion from the site of any person employed thereon.

CDM Regulations – Undertakings to comply[26]

3·9 Each Party acknowledges that he is aware of and undertakes to the other that in relation to the Works and site he will duly comply with the CDM Regulations. Without limitation, where the project that comprises or includes the Works is notifiable:

---

[26] As to the duties imposed by the CDM Regulations 2007, see the Guidance Notes.

continued 3·9

·1 the Employer shall ensure that the CDM Co-ordinator carries out all his duties and, where the Contractor is not the Principal Contractor, shall ensure that the Principal Contractor carries out all his duties under those regulations;

·2 where the Contractor is and while he remains the Principal Contractor, he shall ensure that:

·1 the Construction Phase Plan is prepared and received by the Employer before construction work under this Contract is commenced, and that any subsequent amendment to it by the Contractor is notified to the Employer, the CDM Co-ordinator and (where not the CDM Co-ordinator) the Architect/Contract Administrator; and

·2 welfare facilities complying with Schedule 2 of the CDM Regulations are provided from the commencement of construction work until the end of the construction phase[27];

·3 where the Contractor is not the Principal Contractor, he shall promptly notify the Principal Contractor of the identity of each sub-contractor that he appoints and each sub-subcontractor appointment notified to him;

·4 the Contractor shall promptly upon the written request of the CDM Co-ordinator provide, and shall ensure that any sub-contractor, through the Contractor, provides, to the CDM Co-ordinator (or, if the Contractor is not the Principal Contractor, to the Principal Contractor) such information as the CDM Co-ordinator reasonably requires for the preparation of the health and safety file.

Appointment of successors

3·10 If the Employer by a further appointment replaces the CDM Co-ordinator or the Principal Contractor, the Employer shall immediately upon the further appointment notify the Contractor in writing of the name and address of the new appointee. If the Employer appoints a successor to the Contractor as the Principal Contractor, the Contractor shall at no cost to the Employer comply with all reasonable requirements of the new Principal Contractor to the extent necessary for compliance with the CDM Regulations; no extension of time shall be given in respect of such compliance.

Section 4 Payment

VAT

4·1 The Contract Sum is exclusive of VAT and in relation to any payment to the Contractor under this Contract, the Employer shall in addition pay the amount of any VAT properly chargeable in respect of it.

Construction Industry Scheme (CIS)

4·2 If the Employer is or at any time up to the payment of the final certificate becomes a 'contractor' for the purposes of the CIS[28], his obligation to make any payment under this Contract is subject to the provisions of the CIS.

Progress payments and retention

4·3 The Architect/Contract Administrator shall, at intervals of 4 weeks calculated from the Date for Commencement of the Works, certify progress payments of the percentage stated in the Contract Particulars of the total value of:

---

[27] There is a duty on contractors to ensure compliance with Schedule 2 of the CDM Regulations so far as is reasonably practicable, whether or not the project is notifiable and whether or not the contractor is the Principal Contractor.

[28] See the Contract Particulars (Fourth Recital and clause 4·2).

continued 4·3

·1 work properly executed, including any amounts ascertained or agreed under clauses 3·6 and 3·7; and

·2 materials and goods which have reasonably and properly been brought on to the site for the purpose of the Works and are adequately protected against weather and other casualties

less the amount stated as due to the Contractor in previous progress payment certificates. The certificate shall state the amount due to the Contractor from the Employer, to what the amount relates and the basis on which the amount has been calculated. The final date for payment of the amount certified shall be 14 days from the date of issue of the certificate.

Interim payments on and after practical completion

4·4 The Architect/Contract Administrator shall within 14 days after the date of practical completion of the Works certify payment to be made to the Contractor of the percentage stated in the Contract Particulars of the total amount to be paid to the Contractor under this Contract so far as that amount is ascertainable at the date of practical completion, including any amounts ascertained or agreed under clauses 3·6 and 3·7, less the total amounts due to the Contractor in previous progress payment certificates. Payment certificates shall thereafter be issued at intervals of 2 months (unless otherwise agreed) up to the expiry of the Rectification Period. The certificate shall state the amount due to the Contractor, to what the amount relates and the basis on which the amount has been calculated. The final date for payment of the amount certified shall be 14 days from the date of issue of the certificate.

Notices of amounts to be paid and deductions

4·5 ·1 Not later than 5 days after the date of issue of a payment certificate pursuant to clause 4·3 or 4·4 the Employer shall give a written notice to the Contractor which shall, in respect of the amount stated as due in that certificate, specify the amount of the payment proposed to be made, to what the amount relates and the basis on which the amount has been calculated.

·2 Not later than 5 days before the final date for payment the Employer may give a written notice to the Contractor which shall specify any amount proposed to be withheld or deducted from the amount due, the ground or grounds for such withholding or deduction and the amount of the withholding or deduction attributable to each ground.

·3 Subject to any notice given under clause 4·5·2, the Employer shall no later than the final date for payment pay the Contractor the amount specified in the notice given under clause 4·5·1 or, in the absence of a notice under clause 4·5·1, the amount stated as due in the certificate.

Failure to pay amount due

4·6 If the Employer fails properly to pay the amount, or any part of it, due to the Contractor under clause 4·3 or 4·4 by the final date for its payment, the Employer shall, in addition to the amount not properly paid, pay the Contractor simple interest at the Interest Rate for the period until payment is made. Interest under this clause 4·6 shall be a debt due to the Contractor by the Employer. Acceptance of a payment of interest under this clause 4·6 shall not in any circumstances be construed as a waiver of the Contractor's right to proper payment of the principal amount due, to suspend performance under clause 4·7 or to terminate his employment under section 6.

Contractor's right of suspension

4·7 Without affecting the Contractor's other rights and remedies, if the Employer, subject to any notice issued pursuant to clause 4·5·2, fails to pay the Contractor in full (including any VAT properly chargeable in respect of such payment) by the final date for payment as required by these Conditions and the failure continues for 7 days after the Contractor has given written notice to the Employer, with a copy to the Architect/Contract Administrator, of his intention to suspend performance of his obligations under this Contract and the ground or grounds on which it is intended to suspend performance, the Contractor may suspend such performance until payment is made in full.

Final certificate

4·8 ·1 The Contractor shall within the period stated in the Contract Particulars supply all documentation reasonably required for the computation of the amount to be finally certified by the Architect/Contract Administrator and, provided that the Architect/Contract Administrator has issued the certificate under clause 2·11, the Architect/Contract Administrator shall within 28 days of receipt of such documentation issue a final certificate certifying the amount due to the Contractor or to the Employer, as the case may be. The Final Certificate shall state the basis on which the amount has been calculated.

·2 Not later than 5 days after the date of issue of the final certificate the Party by whom the balance is stated to be payable ('the paying Party') shall give a written notice to the other Party which shall, in respect of any balance stated as due, specify the amount of the payment proposed to be made, to what the amount relates and the basis on which the amount has been calculated.

·3 The final date for payment of the balance shall be 14 days from the date of issue of the final certificate. Not later than 5 days before the final date for payment the paying Party may give a written notice to the other Party which shall specify any amount proposed to be withheld or deducted from any balance due to the other Party, the ground or grounds for such withholding or deduction and the amount of the withholding or deduction attributable to each ground.

·4 Where the paying Party does not give a written notice pursuant to clause 4·8·2 he shall, subject to any notice given under clause 4·8·3, pay the other Party any balance stated as due to the other Party in the final certificate.

Failure to pay final amount

4·9 If the paying Party fails properly to pay the balance, or any part of it, under clause 4·8 by the final date for its payment, he shall in addition to the amount not properly paid pay to the other Party simple interest at the Interest Rate for the period until payment is made. Acceptance of a payment of interest under this clause 4·9 shall not in any circumstances be construed as a waiver of any right to proper payment of the balance.

Fixed price

4·10 Except as provided in clause 4·11, if applicable, no account shall be taken in any payment to the Contractor under this Contract of any change in the cost to the Contractor of the labour, materials, plant and other resources employed in carrying out the Works.

Contribution, levy and tax changes

4·11 If the Contract Particulars state that Schedule 2 (*Fluctuations Option*) applies, contribution, levy and tax changes shall be dealt with by the application of that Schedule. The percentage addition under paragraph 13 of the Schedule is that stated in the Contract Particulars.

Section 5 Injury, Damage and Insurance

Liability of Contractor – personal injury or death

5·1 The Contractor shall be liable for, and shall indemnify the Employer against, any expense, liability, loss, claim or proceedings whatsoever in respect of personal injury to or death of any person arising out of or in the course of or caused by the carrying out of the Works, except to the extent that the same is due to any act or neglect of the Employer or of any person for whom the Employer is responsible.

Liability of Contractor – injury or damage to property

5·2 The Contractor shall be liable for, and shall indemnify the Employer against, any expense, liability, loss, claim or proceedings in respect of any loss, injury or damage whatsoever to any property real or personal (other *continued 5·2* than loss, injury or damage to the Works and/or Site Materials or, where clause 5·4B applies, to any property required to be insured thereunder caused by a Specified Peril) in so far as such loss, injury or damage arises out of or in the course of or by reason of the carrying out of the Works and to the extent that the same is due to any negligence, breach of statutory duty, omission or default of the Contractor or any person employed or engaged by the Contractor on or in connection with the Works or any part of them.

Contractor's insurance of his liability

5·3 Without prejudice to his obligation to indemnify the Employer under clauses 5·1 and 5·2, the Contractor shall take out and maintain (and shall cause any sub-contractor similarly to take out and maintain) insurance in respect of claims arising out of his liability referred to in clauses 5·1 and 5·2 which:

·1 in respect of claims for personal injury to or the death of any employee of the Contractor arising out of and in the course of such person's employment, shall comply with all relevant legislation; and

·2 for all other claims to which clause 5·3 applies[29], shall indemnify the Employer in like manner to the Contractor, but only to the extent that the Contractor may be liable to indemnify the Employer under the terms of this Contract and shall be in a sum not less than that stated in the Contract Particulars for any one occurrence or series of occurrences arising out of one event.

Insurance of the Works by Contractor in Joint Names

5·4A ·1 If the Contract Particulars state that clause 5·4A applies[30], the Contractor shall take out and maintain with insurers approved by the Employer a Joint Names Policy for All Risks Insurance for the full reinstatement value of the Works (plus the percentage, if any, stated in the Contract Particulars to cover professional fees) and shall maintain such Joint Names Policy up to and including the date of issue of the practical completion certificate or, if earlier, the date of termination of the Contractor's employment (whether or not the validity of that termination is contested).

·2 ·1 After any inspection required by the insurers in respect of a claim under the insurance has been completed, the Contractor shall with due diligence restore the damaged work, replace or repair any lost or damaged Site Materials, remove and dispose of any debris and proceed with the carrying out and completion of the Works.

·2 The Contractor shall authorise the insurers to pay all monies from such insurance to the Employer and the Employer may retain from monies paid by the insurers the amount properly incurred by the Employer in respect of professional fees up to an amount which shall not exceed the amount of the percentage additional cover for those fees or (if less) the amount paid by insurers in respect of those fees.

·3 In respect of restoration, replacement or repair of such loss or damage and (when required) the removal and disposal of debris, the Contractor shall not be entitled to any payment other than amounts received under the insurance referred to in clause 5·4A·1 (less only the amount stated in clause 5·4A·2·2) and such amounts shall be paid to the Contractor under certificates of the Architect/Contract Administrator at the intervals stated in clause 4·3.

Insurance of existing structures and the Works by Employer in Joint Names

5·4B ·1 If the Contract Particulars state that clause 5·4B applies, the Employer shall take out and maintain:

·1 a Joint Names Policy in respect of the existing structures together with the contents of them owned by him or for which he is responsible, for the full cost of reinstatement, repair or replacement of loss or damage due to any of the Specified Perils;

·2 a Joint Names Policy for All Risks Insurance for the full reinstatement value of the Works (plus the percentage, if any, stated in the Contract Particulars to cover professional fees)

---

[29] It should be noted that the cover granted under public liability policies taken out pursuant to clause 5·3 may not be co-extensive with the indemnity given to the Employer in clauses 5·1 and 5·2: for example, each claim may be subject to the excess in the policy and cover may not be available in respect of loss or damage due to gradual pollution.

[30] Where the Contractor has in force an All Risks Policy which insures the Works, this Policy may be used to provide the insurance required by clause 5·4A provided the Policy recognises the Employer as a joint insured with the Contractor in respect of the Works and the Policy is maintained. As to full reinstatement value see the Guidance Notes.

continued 5·4B·1

and shall maintain such Joint Names Policies up to and including the date of issue of the practical completion certificate or, if earlier, the date of termination of the Contractor's employment (whether or not the validity of that termination is contested). The Contractor shall authorise the insurers to pay all monies from such insurance to the Employer.

·2 If any loss or damage as referred to in clause 5·4B·1·2 occurs to the Works or to any Site Materials then the Architect/Contract Administrator shall issue instructions under clause 3·4, as are reasonable, for the reinstatement and making good of such loss or damage and such instructions shall be valued under clause 3·6.

Insurance of existing structures by Employer in own name

5·4C If the Contract Particulars state that clause 5·4C applies, the Employer shall, if he has not already done so, take out and maintain in his own name a policy in respect of the existing structures together with the contents thereof owned by him or for which he is responsible, for the full cost of reinstatement, repair or replacement of loss or damage due to any of the Specified Perils up to and including the date of issue of the practical completion certificate or (if earlier) the date of termination of the Contractor's employment (whether or not the validity of that termination is contested).

Evidence of insurance

5·5 The Contractor shall produce, and shall cause any sub-contractor to produce, such evidence as the Employer may reasonably require that the insurances referred to in clause 5·3 and, where applicable, clause 5·4A have been taken out and are in force at all material times. Where clause 5·4B or 5·4C is applicable and except where the Employer is a Local Authority, the Employer shall, as and when reasonably required by the Contractor, produce documentary evidence showing that the insurance referred to therein has been taken out and is being maintained.

Section 6 Termination

Meaning of insolvency

6·1 For the purposes of these Conditions, a Party is Insolvent if:

·1 he enters into an arrangement, compromise or composition in satisfaction of his debts (excluding a scheme of arrangement as a solvent company for the purposes of amalgamation or reconstruction); or

·2 without a declaration of solvency, he passes a resolution or makes a determination that he be wound up; or

·3 he has a winding up order or bankruptcy order made against him; or

·4 he has appointed to him an administrator or administrative receiver; or

·5 (additionally, in the case of a partnership) each partner is the subject of an individual arrangement or any other event or proceedings referred to in clauses 6·1·1 to 6·1·4.

Notices under section 6

6·2 ·1 Notice of termination of the Contractor's employment shall not be given unreasonably or vexatiously.

·2 Such termination shall take effect on receipt of the relevant notice.

·3 Each notice referred to in this section shall be in writing and delivered by hand or sent by Recorded Signed for or Special Delivery post. Where sent by post in that manner, it shall, subject to proof to the contrary, be deemed to have been received on the second Business Day after the date of posting.

Other rights, reinstatement

6·3 ·1 The provisions of clauses 6·4 to 6·7 are without prejudice to any other rights and remedies of the Employer. The provisions of clauses 6·8 and 6·9 and (in the case of termination under either of those clauses) the provisions of clause 6·11, are without prejudice to any other rights and remedies of the Contractor.

·2 Irrespective of the grounds of termination, the Contractor's employment may at any time be reinstated if and on such terms as the Parties agree.

Default by Contractor

6·4 ·1 If, before practical completion of the Works, the Contractor:

·1 without reasonable cause wholly or substantially suspends the carrying out of the Works; or

·2 fails to proceed regularly and diligently with the Works; or

·3 fails to comply with clause 3·9,

the Architect/Contract Administrator may give to the Contractor a notice specifying the default or defaults (the 'specified default or defaults').

·2 If the Contractor continues a specified default for 7 days from receipt of the notice under clause 6·4·1, the Employer may on, or within 10 days from, the expiry of that 7 day period by a further notice to the Contractor terminate the Contractor's employment under this Contract.

Insolvency of Contractor

6·5 ·1 If the Contractor is Insolvent, the Employer may at any time by notice to the Contractor terminate the Contractor's employment under this Contract.

·2 As from the date the Contractor becomes Insolvent, whether or not the Employer has given such notice of termination:

·1 the provisions of clauses 6·7·3 and 6·7·4 shall apply as if such notice had been given and the other provisions of this Contract which require any further payment or any release of Retention shall cease to apply;

·2 the Contractor's obligations under Article 1 and these Conditions to carry out and complete the Works shall be suspended; and

·3 the Employer may take reasonable measures to ensure that the site, the Works and Site Materials are adequately protected and that such Site Materials are retained on site; the Contractor shall allow and shall not hinder or delay the taking of those measures.

Corruption

6·6 The Employer shall be entitled by notice to the Contractor to terminate the Contractor's employment, under this or any other contract with the Employer if, in relation to this or any other such contract, the Contractor or any person employed by him or acting on his behalf shall have committed an offence under the Prevention of Corruption Acts 1889 to 1916, or, where the Employer is a Local Authority, shall have given any fee or reward the receipt of which is an offence under sub-section (2) of section 117 of the Local Government Act 1972.

Consequences of termination under clauses 6·4 to 6·6

6·7 If the Contractor's employment is terminated under clause 6·4, 6·5 or 6·6:

·1 the Employer may employ and pay other persons to carry out and complete the Works, and he and they may enter upon and take possession of the site and the Works and (subject to obtaining any necessary third party consents) may use all temporary buildings, plant, tools, equipment and Site Materials for those purposes;

continued 6·7

·2 (if not already applicable) clauses 6·7·3 and 6·7·4 shall thereupon apply and the other provisions of this Contract which require any further payment or any release of Retention to the Contractor shall cease to apply;

·3 within a reasonable time after the completion of the Works and the making good of defects (or of instructions otherwise, as referred to in clause 2·10), an account of the following shall be set out in a certificate issued by the Architect/Contract Administrator or a statement prepared by the Employer:

·1 the amount of expenses properly incurred by the Employer, including those incurred pursuant to clause 6·7·1 and, where applicable, clause 6·5·2·3, and of any direct loss and/or damage caused to the Employer and for which the Contractor is liable, whether arising as a result of the termination or otherwise;

·2 the amount of payments made to the Contractor; and

·3 the total amount which would have been payable for the Works in accordance with this Contract;

·4 if the sum of the amounts stated under clauses 6·7·3·1 and 6·7·3·2 exceeds the amount stated under clause 6·7·3·3, the difference shall be a debt payable by the Contractor to the Employer or, if that sum is less, by the Employer to the Contractor.

Default by Employer

6·8 ·1 If the Employer:

·1 does not pay by the final date for payment the amount properly due to the Contractor in respect of any certificate and/or any VAT properly chargeable on that amount; or

·2 interferes with or obstructs the issue of any certificate due under this Contract; or

·3 fails to comply with clause 3·9,

the Contractor may give to the Employer a notice specifying the default or defaults (the 'specified default or defaults').

·2 If before practical completion of the Works the carrying out of the whole or substantially the whole of the uncompleted Works is suspended for a continuous period of one month or more by reason of:

·1 Architect/Contract Administrator's instructions under clause 2·4 or 3·6; and/or

·2 any impediment, prevention or default, whether by act or omission, by the Employer, the Architect/Contract Administrator or any person for whom the Employer is responsible

(but in either case excluding such instructions as are referred to in clause 6·10·1·2), then, unless in either case that is caused by the negligence or default of the Contractor or his employees, agents or sub-contractors, the Contractor may give to the Employer a notice specifying the event or events (the 'specified suspension event or events').

·3 If a specified default or a specified suspension event continues for 7 days from the receipt of notice under clause 6·8·1 or 6·8·2, the Contractor may on, or within 10 days from, the expiry of that 7 day period by a further notice to the Employer terminate the Contractor's employment under this Contract.

Insolvency of Employer

6·9 ·1 If the Employer is Insolvent, the Contractor may by notice to the Employer terminate the Contractor's employment under this Contract;

·2 as from the date the Employer becomes Insolvent, the Contractor's obligations under Article 1 and these Conditions to carry out and complete the Works shall be suspended.

Termination by either Party

6·10 ·1 If, before practical completion of the Works, the carrying out of the whole or substantially the whole of the uncompleted Works is suspended for the relevant continuous period of one month or more by reason of one or more of the following events:

·1 force majeure;

·2 Architect/Contract Administrator's instructions under clause 2·4 or 3·6 issued as a result of the negligence or default of any Statutory Undertaker;

·3 loss or damage to the Works occasioned by any of the Specified Perils;

·4 civil commotion or the use or threat of Terrorism and/or the activities of the relevant authorities in dealing with such event or threat; or

·5 the exercise by the United Kingdom Government of any statutory power which directly affects the execution of the Works,

then either Party, subject to clause 6·10·2, may upon the expiry of that relevant period of suspension give notice in writing to the other that, unless the suspension ceases within 7 days after the date of receipt of that notice, he may terminate the Contractor's employment under this Contract. Failing such cessation within that 7 day period, he may then by further notice terminate that employment.

·2 The Contractor shall not be entitled to give notice under clause 6·10·1 in respect of the matter referred to in clause 6·10·1·3 where the loss or damage to the Works occasioned by a Specified Peril was caused by the negligence or default of the Contractor or his employees, agents or sub-contractors.

Consequences of termination under clauses 6·8 to 6·10

6·11 If the Contractor's employment is terminated under any of clauses 6·8 to 6·10:

·1 the provisions of this clause 6·11 shall thereupon apply and the other provisions of this Contract which require any further payment or any release of Retention to the Contractor shall cease to apply;

·2 the Contractor shall as soon as reasonably practicable prepare an account. The account shall set out the amounts referred to in clauses 6·11·2·1 and 6·11·2·2 and, if applicable, clause 6·11·2·3, namely:

·1 the total value of work properly executed at the date of termination of the Contractor's employment, ascertained in accordance with these Conditions as if the employment had not been terminated, together with any other amounts due to the Contractor under these Conditions;

·2 the cost of materials or goods (including Site Materials) properly ordered for the Works for which the Contractor then has paid or is legally bound to pay;

·3 any direct loss and/or damage caused to the Contractor by the termination;

·3 the account shall include the amount, if any, referred to in clause 6·11·2·3 only where the Contractor's employment is terminated either:

·1 under clause 6·8 or 6·9; or

·2 under clause 6·10·1·3, if the loss or damage to the Works occasioned by any of the Specified Perils was caused by the negligence or default of the Employer or any person for whom the Employer is responsible;

·4 after taking into account amounts previously paid to the Contractor under this Contract, the Employer shall pay to the Contractor the amount properly due in respect of the account within 28 days of its submission by the Contractor to the Employer, without deduction of any Retention. Payment by the Employer for any such materials and goods as are referred to in clause 6·11·2·2 shall be subject to such materials and goods thereupon becoming the property of the Employer.

Section 7 Settlement of Disputes

Mediation

7·1 Subject to Article 6, if a dispute or difference arises under this Contract which cannot be resolved by direct negotiations, each Party shall give serious consideration to any request by the other to refer the matter to mediation.

Adjudication

7·2 If a dispute or difference arises under this Contract which either Party wishes to refer to adjudication, the Scheme shall apply except that for the purposes of the Scheme the Adjudicator shall be the person (if any) and the nominating body shall be that stated in the Contract Particulars.

Arbitration

7·3 For the purposes of Article 7, if it applies, the procedures for arbitration are set out in Schedule 1.[31]

---

[31] Arbitration or legal proceedings are **not** an appeal against the decision of the Adjudicator but are a consideration of the dispute or difference as if no decision had been made by an Adjudicator.

Schedules

Schedule 1 Arbitration

(Clause 7·3)

Conduct of arbitration

1 Any arbitration pursuant to Article 7 shall be conducted in accordance with the JCT 2005 edition of the Construction Industry Model Arbitration Rules (CIMAR), provided that if any amendments to that edition of the Rules have been issued by the JCT the Parties may, by a joint notice in writing to the Arbitrator, state that they wish the arbitration to be conducted in accordance with the Rules as so amended. References in this Schedule 1 to a Rule or Rules are references to such Rule(s) as set out in the JCT 2005 edition of CIMAR.

Notice of reference to arbitration

2 ·1 Where pursuant to Article 7 either Party requires a dispute or difference to be referred to arbitration, that Party shall serve on the other Party a written notice of arbitration to such effect in accordance with Rule 2.1 identifying the dispute and requiring the other Party to agree to the appointment of an arbitrator. The Arbitrator shall be an individual agreed by the Parties or, failing such agreement within 14 days (or any agreed extension of that period) after the notice of arbitration is served, appointed on the application of either Party in accordance with Rule 2.3 by the person named in the Contract Particulars.

·2 Where two or more related arbitral proceedings in respect of the Works fall under separate arbitration agreements, Rules 2.6, 2.7 and 2.8 shall apply.

·3 After an arbitrator has been appointed either Party may give a further notice of arbitration to the other Party and to the Arbitrator referring any other dispute which falls under Article 7 to be decided in the arbitral proceedings and Rule 3.3 shall apply.

Powers of Arbitrator

3 Subject to the provisions of Article 7 the Arbitrator shall, without prejudice to the generality of his powers, have power to rectify this Contract so that it accurately reflects the true agreement made by the Parties, to direct such measurements and/or valuations as may in his opinion be desirable in order to determine the rights of the Parties and to ascertain and award any sum which ought to have been the subject of or included in any certificate and to open up, review and revise any certificate, opinion, decision, requirement or notice and to determine all matters in dispute which shall be submitted to him in the same manner as if no such certificate, opinion, decision, requirement or notice had been given.

Effect of award

4 Subject to paragraph 5 the award of the Arbitrator shall be final and binding on the Parties.

Appeal – questions of law

5 The Parties hereby agree pursuant to section 45(2)(a) and section 69(2)(a) of the Arbitration Act 1996 that either Party may (upon notice to the other Party and to the Arbitrator):

·1 apply to the courts to determine any question of law arising in the course of the reference, and

·2 appeal to the courts on any question of law arising out of an award made in an arbitration under this arbitration agreement.

Arbitration Act 1996

6 The provisions of the Arbitration Act 1996 shall apply to any arbitration under this Contract wherever the same, or any part of it, shall be conducted.

Schedule 2 Fluctuations Option – Contribution, levy and tax changes

(Clause 4·11)

Deemed calculation of Contract Sum – labour

1 The Contract Sum shall be deemed to have been calculated in the manner set out below and shall be subject to adjustment in the events specified hereunder.

·1 The Contract Sum is based upon the types and rates of contribution, levy and tax payable by a person in his capacity as an employer and which at the Base Date are payable by the Contractor. A type and a rate so payable are in paragraph 1·2 referred to as a 'tender type' and a 'tender rate'.

·2 If any of the tender rates other than a rate of levy payable by virtue of the Industrial Training Act 1982 is increased or decreased, or if a tender type ceases to be payable, or if a new type of contribution, levy or tax which is payable by a person in his capacity as an employer becomes payable after the Base Date, then in any such case the net amount of the difference between what the Contractor actually pays or will pay in respect of:

·1 workpeople engaged upon or in connection with the Works either on or adjacent to the site; and

·2 workpeople directly employed by the Contractor who are engaged upon the production of materials or goods for use in or in connection with the Works and who operate neither on nor adjacent to the site and to the extent that they are so engaged

or because of his employment of such workpeople and what he would have paid had the alteration, cessation or new type of contribution, levy or tax not become effective shall, as the case may be, be paid to or allowed by the Contractor.

·3 There shall be added to the net amount paid to or allowed by the Contractor under paragraph 1·2, in respect of each person employed by the Contractor who is engaged upon or in connection with the Works either on or adjacent to the site and who is not within the definition of workpeople in paragraph 12·3, the same amount as is payable or allowable in respect of a craftsman under paragraph 1·2 or such proportion of that amount as reflects the time (measured in whole working days) that each such person is so employed.

·4 For the purposes of paragraph 1·3:

·1 no period of less than 2 whole working days in any week shall be taken into account and periods of less than a whole working day shall not be aggregated to amount to a whole working day;

·2 "the same amount as is payable or allowable in respect of a craftsman" shall refer to the amount in respect of a craftsman employed by the Contractor (or by any sub-contractor under a sub-contract to which paragraph 3 refers) under the rules or decisions or agreements of the Construction Industry Joint Council or other wage-fixing body and, where those rules or decisions or agreements provide for more than one rate of wage, emolument or other expense for a craftsman, shall refer to the amount in respect of a craftsman employed as aforesaid to whom the highest rate is applicable; and

·3 "employed by the Contractor" shall mean an employment to which the Income Tax (Pay As You Earn) Regulations 2003 apply.

continued 1

·5 The Contract Sum is based upon the types and rates of refund of the contributions, levies and taxes payable by a person in his capacity as an employer and upon the types and rates of premium receivable by a person in his capacity as an employer being in each case types and rates which at the Base Date are receivable by the Contractor. Such a type and such a rate are in paragraph 1·6 referred to as a 'tender type' and a 'tender rate'.

·6 If any of the tender rates is increased or decreased or if a tender type ceases to be payable or if a new type of refund of any contribution, levy or tax payable by a person in his capacity as an employer becomes receivable or if a new type of premium receivable by a person in his capacity as an employer becomes receivable after the Base Date, then in any such case the net amount of the difference between what the Contractor actually receives or will receive in respect of workpeople as referred to in paragraphs 1·2·1 and 1·2·2 or because of his employment of such workpeople and what he would have received had the alteration, cessation or new type of refund or premium not become effective shall, as the case may be, be paid to or allowed by the Contractor.

·7 The references in paragraphs 1·5 and 1·6 to premiums shall be construed as meaning all payments howsoever they are described which are made under or by virtue of an Act of Parliament to a person in his capacity as an employer and which affect the cost to an employer of having persons in his employment.

·8 Where employer's contributions are payable by the Contractor in respect of workpeople as referred to in paragraphs 1·2·1 and 1·2·2 whose employment is contracted-out employment within the meaning of the Pension Schemes Act 1993, the Contractor shall for the purpose of recovery or allowance under paragraph 1 be deemed to pay employer's contributions as if that employment were not contracted-out employment.

·9 The references in paragraph 1 to contributions, levies and taxes shall be construed as meaning all impositions payable by a person in his capacity as an employer howsoever they are described and whoever the recipient which are imposed under or by virtue of an Act of Parliament and which affect the cost to an employer of having persons in his employment.

Deemed calculation of Contract Sum – materials

2 The Contract Sum shall be deemed to have been calculated in the manner set out below and shall be subject to adjustment in the events specified hereunder.

·1 The Contract Sum is based upon the types and rates of duty, if any, and tax, if any (other than any VAT which is treated, or is capable of being treated, as input tax by the Contractor), by whomsoever payable which at the Base Date are payable on the import, purchase, sale, appropriation, processing, use or disposal of the materials, goods, electricity, fuels, materials taken from the site as waste or any other solid, liquid or gas necessary for the execution of the Works by virtue of any Act of Parliament. A type and a rate so payable are in paragraph 2·2 referred to as a 'tender type' and a 'tender rate'.

·2 If, in relation to any materials or goods or any electricity or fuels or materials taken from the site as waste or any other solid, liquid or gas necessary for the execution of the Works including temporary site installations for those Works, a tender rate is increased or decreased or a tender type ceases to be payable or a new type of duty or tax (other than any VAT which is treated, or is capable of being treated, as input tax by the Contractor) becomes payable on the import, purchase, sale, appropriation, processing, use or disposal of any of the above things after the Base Date, then in any such case the net amount of the difference between what the Contractor actually pays in respect of those materials, goods, electricity, fuels, materials taken from the site as waste or any other solid, liquid or gas and what he would have paid in respect of them had the alteration, cessation or imposition not occurred shall, as the case may be, be paid to or allowed by the Contractor. In this paragraph 2·2 "a new type of duty or tax" includes an additional duty or tax and a duty or tax imposed in regard to any of the above in respect of which no duty or tax whatever was previously payable (other than any VAT which is treated, or is capable of being treated, as input tax by the Contractor).

Sub-contract work – incorporation of provisions to like effect

3 ·1 If the Contractor sub-contracts any portion of the Works he shall incorporate in the sub-contract provisions to the like effect as the provisions of this Fluctuations Option (excluding this paragraph 3)

continued 3·1 including the percentage stated in the Contract Particulars pursuant to paragraph 13 which are applicable for the purposes of this Contract.

·2 If the price payable under such a sub-contract as referred to in paragraph 3·1 is increased above or decreased below the price in such sub-contract by reason of the operation of the said incorporated provisions, then the net amount of such increase or decrease shall, as the case may be, be paid to or allowed by the Contractor under this Contract.

Notification by Contractor

4 ·1 The Contractor shall notify the Architect/Contract Administrator in writing of the occurrence of any of the events referred to in such of the following provisions as are applicable for the purposes of this Contract:

·1 paragraph 1·2;

·2 paragraph 1·6;

·3 paragraph 2·2;

·4 paragraph 3·2.

·2 Any notification required to be given under paragraph 4·1 shall be given within a reasonable time after the occurrence of the event to which it relates, and notification in that time shall be a condition precedent to any payment being made to the Contractor in respect of the event in question.

Agreement – Architect/Contract Administrator and Contractor

5 The Architect/Contract Administrator and the Contractor may agree what shall be deemed for all the purposes of this Contract to be the net amount payable to or allowable by the Contractor in respect of the occurrence of any event such as is referred to in any of the provisions listed in paragraph 4·1.

Fluctuations added to or deducted from Contract Sum

6 Any amount which from time to time becomes payable to or allowable by the Contractor by virtue of paragraphs 1 and 2 or paragraph 3 shall, as the case may be, be added to or deducted from the Contract Sum. The addition or deduction to which this paragraph 6 refers shall be subject to the provisions of paragraphs 7 to 10·1.

Evidence and computations by Contractor

7 As soon as is reasonably practicable the Contractor shall provide such evidence and computations as the Architect/Contract Administrator may reasonably require to enable the amount payable to or allowable by the Contractor by virtue of paragraphs 1 and 2 or paragraph 3 to be ascertained; and in the case of amounts payable to or allowable by the Contractor under paragraph 1·3 (or paragraph 3 for amounts payable to or allowable under the provisions in the sub-contract to the like effect as paragraphs 1·3 and 1·4) – employees other than workpeople – such evidence shall include a certificate signed by or on behalf of the Contractor each week certifying the validity of the evidence reasonably required to ascertain such amounts.

Actual payment by Contractor

8 No amount shall be added or deducted in the computation of the amount stated as due in progress payments by virtue of this paragraph 8 unless on or before the date as at which the total value of work, materials and goods is ascertained for the purposes of any progress payment the Contractor shall have actually paid or received the sum which is payable by or to him in consequence of the event in respect of which the payment or allowance arises.

No alteration to Contractor's profit

9 No addition to or deduction from the Contract Sum made by virtue of paragraph 6 shall alter in any way the amount of profit of the Contractor included in that Sum.

Position where Contractor in default over completion

10 ·1 Subject to the provisions of paragraph 10·2 no amount shall be added or deducted in the computation of the amount stated as due in progress payments or in the final certificate in respect of amounts otherwise payable to or allowable by the Contractor by virtue of paragraphs 1 and 2 or paragraph 3 if the event (as referred to in the provisions listed in paragraph 4·1) in respect of which the payment or allowance would be made occurs after the Date for Completion stated in the Contract Particulars or after any later Date for Completion fixed under clause 2·7.

·2 Paragraph 10·1 shall not be applied unless:

·1 the printed text of clause 2·7 is unamended and forms part of the Conditions; and

·2 the Architect/Contract Administrator has, in respect of every notification by the Contractor under clause 2·7, fixed or confirmed in writing such Date for Completion as he considers to be in accordance with that clause.

Work etc. to which paragraphs 1 to 3 not applicable

11 Paragraphs 1 to 3 shall not apply in respect of:

·1 work for which the Contractor is allowed daywork rates under clause 3·6;

·2 changes in the rate of VAT charged on the supply of goods or services by the Contractor to the Employer under this Contract.

Definitions

12 In this Fluctuations Option:

·1 the Base Date means the date stated as such in the Contract Particulars;

·2 "materials" and "goods" include timber used in formwork but do not include other consumable stores, plant and machinery;

·3 "workpeople" means persons whose rates of wages and other emoluments (including holiday credits) are governed by the rules or decisions or agreements of the Construction Industry Joint Council or some other wage-fixing body for trades associated with the building industry;

·4 "wage-fixing body" means a body which lays down recognised terms and conditions of workers;

·5 "recognised terms and conditions" means terms and conditions of workers in comparable employment in the trade or industry, or section of trade or industry, in which the employer in question is engaged which have been settled by an agreement or award to which the parties are employers' associations and independent trade unions which represent (generally, or in the district in question, as the case may be) a substantial proportion of the employers and of the workers in the trade, industry or section being workers of the description to which the agreement or award relates.

Percentage addition to fluctuation payments or allowances

13 There shall be added to the amount paid to or allowed by the Contractor under:

·1 paragraph 1·2,

·2 paragraph 1·3,

·3 paragraph 1·6,

·4 paragraph 2·2

the percentage stated in the Contract Particulars.

Schedule 3 Supplemental Provisions

(Seventh Recital)

Each provision applies unless otherwise stated in the Contract Particulars.

Collaborative working

1 The Parties shall work with each other and with other project team members in a co-operative and collaborative manner, in good faith and in a spirit of trust and respect. To that end, each shall support collaborative behaviour and address behaviour which is not collaborative.

Health and safety

2 ·1 Without limiting either Party's statutory and/or regulatory duties and responsibilities and/or the specific health and safety requirements of this Contract, the Parties will endeavour to establish and maintain a culture and working environment in which health and safety is of paramount concern to everybody involved with the project.

·2 In addition to the specific health and safety requirements of this Contract, the Contractor undertakes to:

·1 comply with any and all approved codes of practice produced or promulgated by the Health and Safety Executive and/or the Health and Safety Commission;

·2 ensure that all personnel engaged by the Contractor and members of the Contractor's supply chain on site receive appropriate site-specific health and safety induction training and regular refresher training;

·3 ensure that all such personnel have access at all times to competent health and safety advice in accordance with regulation 7 of the Management of Health and Safety at Work Regulations 1999; and

·4 ensure that there is full and proper health and safety consultation with all such personnel in accordance with the Health and Safety (Consultation with Employees) Regulations 1996.

Cost savings and value improvements

3 ·1 The Contractor is encouraged to propose changes to designs and specifications for the Works and/or to the programme for their execution that may benefit the Employer, whether in the form of a reduction in the cost of the Works or their associated life cycle costs, through practical completion at a date earlier than the date for completion or otherwise.

·2 The Contractor shall provide details of his proposed changes, identifying them as suggested under this paragraph 3, together with his assessment of the benefit he believes the Employer may obtain, expressed in financial terms, and a quotation.

·3 Where the Employer wishes to implement a change proposed by the Contractor, the Parties shall negotiate with a view to agreeing its value, the financial benefit and any adjustment to the date for completion. Upon agreement, the change and the amount of any adjustment of the Contract Sum shall be confirmed in an Architect/Contract Administrator's instruction, together with the share of the financial benefit to be paid to the Contractor and any adjustment to the date for completion.

·4 Original proposals by the Contractor under this paragraph 3 may only be instructed in accordance with it, provided always that nothing shall prevent the Employer from utilising other contractors to implement such changes after practical completion of the Works.

Sustainable development and environmental considerations

4 ·1 The Contractor is encouraged to suggest economically viable amendments to the Works which, if instructed as a Variation, may result in an improvement in environmental performance in the carrying out of the Works or of the completed Works.

·2 The Contractor shall provide to the Employer all information that he reasonably requests regarding the environmental impact of the supply and use of materials and goods which the Contractor selects.

Performance Indicators and monitoring

5 ·1 The Employer shall monitor and assess the Contractor's performance by reference to any performance indicators stated or identified in the Contract Documents.

·2 The Contractor shall provide to the Employer all information that he may reasonably require to monitor and assess the Contractor's performance against the targets for those performance indicators.

·3 Where the Employer considers that a target for any of those performance indicators may not be met, he may inform the Contractor who shall submit his proposals for improving his performance against that target to the Employer.

Notification and negotiation of disputes

6 With a view to avoidance or early resolution of disputes or differences (subject to Article 6), each Party shall promptly notify the other of any matter that appears likely to give rise to a dispute or difference. The senior executives nominated in the Contract Particulars (or if either is not available, a colleague of similar standing) shall meet as soon as practicable for direct, good faith negotiations to resolve the matter.

Guidance Notes

Use of Minor Works Building Contract

1 The Contract should only be used where the employer has engaged an architect or other professionally qualified person to advise on and administer its terms.

2 The criteria for determining the suitability of the Contract are set out on the inside of the front cover.

3 For Works which do not fulfil these criteria, reference should be made to www.jctcontracts.com for guidance as to the appropriate contract to be used.

4 The Contract is predicated upon the lump sum offer obtained being based on drawings and/or a specification and/or work schedules but without detailed measurements. Those documents should therefore be in a form sufficient to enable the Contractor accurately to identify the Works to be done without the provision of bills of quantities by the Employer.

5 The Contract is not suitable for use where the Works are of a complex nature or where the period required for the execution of the Works is such that full labour and materials fluctuation provisions are required.

6 The Contract complies with the requirements of the Housing Grants, Construction and Regeneration Act 1996 in providing for adjudication and certain payment provisions. However, not all building contracts are subject to this Act; for example, a contract with a residential occupier within the meaning of section 106 of the Act is excluded and therefore it does not need to contain adjudication provisions, but, unless amendments are made, a residential occupier in entering into a Minor Works Building Contract will be accepting adjudication as a means of resolving disputes.

7 For some projects where it is intended to use the Contract, the Employer may wish to seek to control the selection of sub-contractors for specialist work. This may be done by naming a person or company in the tender documents or in instructions on the expenditure of a Provisional Sum but there are no provisions in the Contract which deal with the consequences of such naming. Such control of selection may be better achieved by the Employer entering into a direct contract with the specialist.

Outline of the Contract

Architect/Contract Administrator

8 This is the person whom the Employer has engaged to advise on and administer the Contract. If the Employer engages a professional who is not an architect, that person is taken to be referred to in the Contract as the 'Contract Administrator'. Whether the professional is an 'Architect' or a 'Contract Administrator', his/her duties under the Contract are the same.

Role of the Architect/Contract Administrator

9 The Architect/Contract Administrator is paid by the Employer and advises the Employer on all matters in connection with the building work and administers the Contract on behalf of the Employer; however in the following matters he acts independently as between the Employer and the Contractor:

- in issuing payment certificates;
- in valuing any variations or any work instructed in respect of Provisional Sums (see "Terms used") included in the Contract Documents;
- in giving any extension to the time stated in the Contract Particulars for the completion of the building work;
- in certifying the date of practical completion (see "Terms used") and the date when in his opinion all defects which appear during the Rectification Period (see "Terms used") have been made good.

Instructions

10 Under the Contract only the Architect/Contract Administrator can issue instructions to the Contractor; although the Employer is paying for the building work he is not entitled to give any instructions direct to the Contractor in connection with it. If the Employer wishes to make any change to the work or the manner in which it is being carried out, he must ask the Architect/Contract Administrator to give the necessary instructions to the Contractor.

Price

11 This is the lump sum stated in the Contract plus any VAT properly chargeable on the building work. This lump sum may be increased or decreased depending on any changes to the work or the order or period in which it is carried out, the value of work in respect of any Provisional Sums included in the Contract Documents, as instructed by the Architect/Contract Administrator, and, where applicable, any increase and decrease in contributions, levies and taxes for which the Contractor is liable.

Payment

12 Payment is made under certificates issued by the Architect/Contract Administrator every 4 weeks calculated from the date of commencement until practical completion. A further certificate is issued within 14 days of practical completion. Payment certificates are thereafter issued at intervals of 2 months (unless otherwise agreed) up to the expiry of the Retification Period. The final balance is paid following the issue of the final certificate. The final date for payment of certificates, together with any VAT chargeable to the Employer, is 14 days from the date of the issue of the certificate.

Until practical completion, payment certificates will reflect the Employer's entitlement to retain 5 per cent unless a percentage for payment other than 95 per cent is inserted in the Contract Particulars for clause 4·3. The Contract envisages that between practical completion and the final certificate the percentage retained will be halved.

If the Employer fails to pay an amount due to the Contractor by the final date for its payment, interest at a rate of 5% per annum over the official dealing rate of the Bank of England is payable by the Employer for the period until payment is made.

Time-scale for the work

13 If the work cannot be finished within the original time stated in the Contract Particulars for reasons beyond the control of the Contractor, the Architect/Contract Administrator is required to give such extension of time as is reasonable.

The Employer can recover liquidated damages (see "Terms used") from the Contractor if the work is not finished by the Date for Completion (see "Terms used") having taken into account any extension of time.

Suspension

14 If the Employer does not pay the amount due to the Contractor by the final date for its payment, the Contractor can, after giving notice, suspend performance of his obligations under the Contract until payment of that amount is made.

Termination

15 Either Party may end the Contractor's employment if the other Party does not comply with certain stated obligations or if one of the Parties becomes insolvent.

Dealing with disputes

16 Disputes are dealt with either by arbitration, if selected in the Contract Particulars, or through the courts. The Parties may also agree to mediate a dispute. Either Party may also refer any dispute for a 'fast track' decision by an adjudicator; such decision is binding unless and until the dispute is decided by an arbitrator or the court. Residential occupiers wishing to use the Contract should also refer to paragraph 6 above. The Contract Particulars enable the Parties to nominate an individual adjudicator in advance, should they wish.

However, an individual should not be named in the Contract without his prior agreement. It has also to be recognised that those of sufficient standing to merit nomination are generally busy people and that when a dispute arises they may not be available.

The JCT 2005 edition of the Construction Industry Model Arbitration Rules (CIMAR) includes the JCT Supplementary and Advisory Procedures and these will govern any arbitration that is commenced. It is recommended that anyone considering instituting arbitration proceedings should obtain a copy of the rules and, as with litigation, should take competent professional advice before taking steps to institute those proceedings.

In making the choice between arbitration and litigation one should consider, in addition to the existence of adjudication, a range of other factors. Arbitration provides the ability to choose an arbitrator from any relevant profession, greater freedom of choice procedurally and confidentiality, whereas in litigation there is the wider power of the court.

Rights and remedies generally

17 Statutory and common law rights are not restricted by the terms of the Contract. The limitation period for a contract that is simply signed by the Parties is 6 years from the date of the breach or, where it is executed as a deed, 12 years. The limitation period should not be confused with the Rectification Period, which is provided to facilitate the remedying of the Contractor's defective work by allowing him to return to site to make good.

Supplemental Provisions

18 Schedule 3 comprises six optional provisions for use, as appropriate. The use of those provisions will depend upon the scope of the project, the participants and the type of relationship that the Parties wish to have. The choice as to which of the provisions apply is made in the Contract Particulars. If no choice is made the relevant provision will apply. The Supplemental Provisions are generally intended to be disapplied only where there is a Framework Agreement or other contract documentation that covers the same ground.

Terms used

19 The Architect/Contract Administrator should, as part of his duties to the Employer, be prepared to explain the general meanings of the various terms used in the Contract. For example:

Assignment

20 The transfer of rights under the Contract by one Party to a third person. For example, the Contractor may transfer (assign) his rights to payment to 'X'; the Employer, if notified, will then be required to pay 'X' instead of the Contractor.

Base Date

21 The Base Date is stated in the Contract Particulars and is often about 7 days before the date for submission of tenders. The main purpose of the Base Date is determining what fluctuations are payable. In setting it a short period before the tender submission date, tenderers are relieved of trying to deal in that submission with last minute changes.

CDM Regulations

22 Regulations made under Act of Parliament to improve health and safety standards on construction sites. The extent to which the CDM Regulations apply depends on whether or not the project that comprises or includes the Works is notifiable under the CDM Regulations. Part 2 of the CDM Regulations 2007 imposes duties (e.g. as to competence, co-operation, co-ordination and preventive steps) on clients, designers, contractors and sub-contractors at each level, whether or not the project is notifiable, as does Part 4 in relation to contractors, sub-contractors and others controlling work during the construction period. The additional duties contained in Part 3 (including those relating to the CDM Co-ordinator and Principal Contractor) apply only where the project is notifiable. Domestic clients (i.e. clients not acting in the course or furtherance of business) are not subject to duties under the CDM Regulations in relation to purely domestic projects, which in turn are treated as non-notifiable.

CDM Co-ordinator

23 The person named as the CDM Co-ordinator in the Articles of Agreement or subsequently appointed as such as required by the CDM Regulations. A CDM Co-ordinator is required only where the project is notifiable under the CDM Regulations.

Date for Completion

24 The date by which the Contractor is required to finish the work. This is the date stated in the Contract Particulars or as extended by the Architect/Contract Administrator.

Date of practical completion

25 The date certified by the Architect/Contract Administrator when in his opinion the Contractor actually finishes the work to all practical intents and purposes.

Rectification Period

26 The Rectification Period is 3 months from the date of practical completion unless otherwise agreed. Defects in the work which appear during the Rectification Period are required to be put right by the Contractor before he is entitled to be paid the balance of the monies due to him under the Contract.

Health and safety file

27 A manual which the CDM Co-ordinator has to ensure is delivered to the Employer on completion of the work, giving information for the future on the management of health and safety in the maintenance, repair, renovation, occupancy or demolition of the work and its contents. It is only required where the project is notifiable under the CDM Regulations and is not required where the client is a residential occupier undertaking a purely domestic project.

Insurance in Joint Names

28 A policy of insurance under which both Parties are covered if certain events occur. It is difficult to obtain Joint Names insurance for existing structures and contents in those cases that involve residential occupiers. Where such Joint Names insurance is unavailable, the alternative of taking out insurance in the Employer's name (clause 5·4C) should be selected. Where such insurance is already provided under an existing household policy, the Employer's household insurer must nevertheless be notified that building works are to be carried out. The insurer may require the Employer to pay an additional premium. In circumstances where clause 5·4C is to apply clause 5·4A should also remain operative so that the Contractor is required to insure the Works in Joint Names.

29 Each Party should obtain advice from his own insurance adviser about coverage of the risks stated in the Contract. This should be done before the Contract is signed.

30 Any excesses under a policy are normally borne by the Party required to take out the insurance. Care should be taken in determining the full reinstatement value and/or replacement value (including any applicable VAT) for insurance purposes and ensure that the policy includes the removal of debris arising from loss or damage to the Works.

Liquidated damages

31 The rate per day/week/month stated in the Contract Particulars by the Employer, to compensate him for the Contractor's failure to finish the work on time. The rate should be a genuine pre-estimate by the Employer of the financial loss that he is likely to suffer. It is for the Employer to decide whether to deduct any liquidated damages that he might be entitled to from any amount certified as due to the Contractor; such deduction is not taken into account by the Architect/Contract Administrator in the calculation of any certificate.

Provisional Sum

32 A sum included for work which the Employer may or may not decide to have carried out, or which cannot be accurately specified in the original contract documents. For instance, the pricing documents may say "Allow £X for complete external redecoration of the premises." In the event, the Employer may decide to have all, some or none of the outside of the premises re-decorated. If redecoration is wanted by the Employer, the specification required is instructed by the Architect/Contract Administrator and the price to be paid is

either agreed between the Architect/Contract Administrator and the Contractor or valued by the Architect/Contract Administrator.

Variation

33 A change to the work ordered by the Architect/Contract Administrator on behalf of the Employer. The Variation may be an addition to or an omission from the originally specified work or the order or period in which it is carried out.

Revision 2 changes

The following provisions in Revision 2 2009 contain textual changes. The provisions with substantive textual changes have been identified with *.

Revision 2 2009 numbering

Recitals
Sixth*
Seventh*

Articles
Article 7*

Contract Particulars (entries)
Sixth Recital*
Seventh Recital and Schedule 3*
Article 7
4·4
4·8·1*
7·2

Conditions (clauses)
1·2*
1·6*
2·1·2
2·3
2·4
2·7
2·8·2
3·3·1, 3·3·2 introduction*, 3·3·2·3*
3·4
3·6·3*
3·9·1, 3·9·3, 3·9·4
4·2
4·3·1, 4·3·2, 4·3 hanging paragraph*
4·4*
4·5
4·6*
4·7*
4·8*
4·9*
4·11
5·4A·2·3
6·2·3
6·3·2
6·11·2
7·1*

Schedules
Schedule 2 paragraph 3·1
paragraph 4
paragraph 10·2·2
Schedule 3*

MW User Checklist

A checklist of the key information that will help you to complete the Articles of Agreement may be downloaded from the JCT website.
